Gretel II Disqualified

The untold inside story of a famous America's Cup incident

By

B. Devereux Barker III

Assisted by John N. Fiske Jr.

ISBN: 1481999214
ISBN 13: 9781481999212

Library of Congress Control Number: 2013901088
CreateSpace Independent Publishing Platform
North Charleston, South Carolina

Chapter 1

In the early afternoon of September 20, 1970, I became embroiled in something of an international controversy that involved, at least to some degree, every human being who had ever formed an opinion about anything...or so it seemed. An incident – at the very start of the second race of the America's Cup Regatta – not only generated significant passions around the world, but also resulted in a fundamental change in the way America's Cup racing was thereafter adjudicated.

As a youngster, sailing and racing small boats was a significant factor in my life. I spent summers in Marblehead, Massachusetts. Most of my waking hours were on the water or at the Pleon and Eastern Yacht Clubs. In my late teens I was Treasurer and then Commodore of the Pleon YC, America's oldest youth sailing club, run entirely by its under-21 officers and membership.

After graduating from Harvard in 1960, I served a two-year stint in the Navy, stationed at the Naval Academy in Annapolis, administrating and coaching in the well-established and extensive sailing program. In contrast to the small boat sailing with which I had been involved in Marblehead, this provided my first sustained exposure to larger boats and offshore sailing.

In June, 1962, immediately upon being released from active duty, I found myself aboard the 12-Meter defense-candidate *Easterner*, as a winch grinder. *Easterner,* named after the Eastern YC, was always considered the handsomest of Twelves with her varnished mahogany topsides.

Easterner in 1962

My grandfather, B. Devereux Barker, had been a successful racing skipper on a variety of yachts, and had gained some renown in sailing circles. He was surely a factor in my being selected for *Easterner's* crew because I had never before sailed with the Chandler Hovey family who owned her, the designer Ray Hunt or the skipper, George O'Day.

In the opinions of many observers, the ten America's Cup challenges between 1958 and 1987 during which the Cup was raced in the 12-Meter Class were the halcyon years of the Cup. Twelves, in their time, were the ultimate, refined racing yacht. Approximately 70 feet in overall length, with tall rigs, elegant lines and then-still-amateur crews, they were the finest, most easily understood class ever to race for the America's Cup, and the non-sailing public gradually became more and more interested.

Aboard *Easterner,* even though we were not particularly competitive, I enjoyed Newport's sailing and social scene, used new muscles, and for the first time, immersed myself in America's Cup 12-Meter sailing. It was an awakening. Sailing, hockey and baseball were the sports of my youth; now I was a Navy veteran, and in the biggest, big league in international sailing. I loved the intensity and the excellence of the people with whom I was involved. Little did I expect that the summer of 1962 in *Easterner* would set me on a trajectory that led to totally unexpected notoriety.

Although I grew up in Marblehead, the New York Yacht Club had always figured prominently in my family. Both my father and my grandfather were members, and it was only natural that I join also. And I did in 1961. (In 1991, I became a life member of the NYYC. In 2012, I was #42 in seniority in the 3,000-member organization.)

During the summer of 1965, I came into contact with the NYYC Race Committee while covering the finish of the Annapolis – Newport Race at Castle Hill Light for *Yachting* magazine whose editorial staff I had joined after the summer of '62. A large group of boats was finishing together at night in foggy conditions and the committee was struggling to identify them. Since I knew many of the boats by sight, I offered to help and called boat names when sail numbers could not be spotted.

The following year, Chairman Bill Fanning asked me to join the committee, much to my surprise and pleasure. Bill was a great character, full of good stories and wisdom from many years of committee work. He had a sharp eye and could tell when a starting line was square or which end was favored just by looking at a flag. (I always had to use a hand bearing compass.) He became a wonderfully supportive mentor. Although he stepped down as Chairman before the 1967 Cup summer, Bill remained on the committee through my tenure and beyond. One of the ongoing strengths of the NYYC Race Committee was that it had a substantial number of very experienced members. It was widely known to run the best races anywhere.

For 1967, Harry Anderson took over as Chairman. Harry has become a true legend in the sport. To list all of his accomplishments and involvements here would double the size of this book. A few highlights: He served a cumulative total of 139 years as a flag officer, including Commodore of both the NYYC and Seawanhaka Corinthian YC. He served as unpaid Executive Director of the NAYRU (now US Sailing) for 12 years and was on the Appeals Committee for 25 years, establishing himself as a racing rules authority. For eight years he was a vice president of the International Yacht Racing Union. He was Chairman of the American Sail Training Association, now known as Tall Ships America. Harry was heavily involved in college sailing at Yale, both during his undergraduate years and to this day. He was also instrumental in advancing the sport of sailing at the University of Rhode Island and for his efforts was awarded an honorary degree. For many years he was on the advisory Fales Committee at the US Naval Academy. It goes on and on.

Anderson made me Secretary of the committee, a sort of second in command, as soon as he became Chairman. There were probably more than a few doubts about the appointment because of my youth and relative lack of experience, but none of the more senior committee members resigned, a good indication that they were okay with the choice. I recall 1967 as an easy, enjoyable summer. The committee functioned normally and smoothly and, for the most part, the weather cooperated. The newly-built *Intrepid* defended easily in four straight by large margins against Australia's *Dame Pattie*.

After the 1968 season, Harry suggested to me that I was ready to be chairman of the Race Committee and he apparently was able to so convince the club's Nominating Committee. Now, in 1969, I was only 30. I had a full time job as an editor at *Yachting* (which fortuitously was located across 44th Street from the Club), two young children, but barely sufficient experience, in my opinion, to manage a major sports event that included the world's most important sailboat races. But it was a challenge I relished. I was confident that with hard work and attention to detail, a tradition of running excellent races would be preserved. And we had a superb Race Committee.

The New York Yacht Club's regular Race Committee in 1970 consisted of: the afore-mentioned **Willis "Bill" Fanning** who kept us all alert and happy, **Bill Foulk** who became my successor, ran the '74 Cup and was for six years a member of the US Sailing Racing Rules Appeals Committee, **Charlie Adams** from a longtime sailing family, who I brought to the committee along with Foulk ; **Jim Carroll,** also new to the NYYC Race Committee with tons of experience running races for Marblehead's Eastern YC and in Bermuda, **Wes Oliver** who served 1965-1983 and whose name-sake son became a chairman, and **Henry Scholtz** of Riverside (CT) YC who had *two* sons that later became NYYC Race Chairmen. I had enormous respect for all the other Committeemen, some of whom were more than twice my age. They accepted me as their leader, and, as it turned out later, their voice to the world.

1970 NYYC Race Committee (l. to r.) Charlie Adams, Bill Foulk, Henry Scholtz, Bill Fanning, Jim Carroll, Wes Oliver, Dev Barker

In a normal year, the seven-man committee could handle everything, but a Cup summer was a different story. We needed a dozen members to run a Cup race. We were "on-station" for 63 days. Remember, nobody was being paid. All of these men were volunteers. If they were of working age, they held down paying jobs. When their wives and children were to be in Newport, they had to find their own housing.

We had an able and talented Auxiliary Race Committee in 1970 as well:

Joe Bartram handled our boat charters and continued a family tradition of Syndicate management.

Jerry Bliss, longtime regular member who ran more races at Edgartown than anybody, ever.

Bill Burnham, another experienced former regular who kept us well fed.

CDR Dick Dermody, USN, handled liaison with Navy which provided tugs at marks.

Jack Dickerson among the best ever, great character, NYYC chairman 1955 to 1958.

LCDR Toby Field, USN, avid Newport racer groomed to take over from Dermody.

Dick Goennel, foredeck on *Constellation* in '64, *Yachting* advertising salesman.

Don King, the dean of Long Island Sound committeemen, from Larchmont, NY.

Charlie Morgan served in every Cup summer '58 to '83, son of America's Cup Committee chairman.

Roger Schultz, worked at CBS, helpful in obtaining assistance from Walter Cronkite.

Charlie Schulz, newly recruited expert in communications and accurate mark positioning.

Bob Wessmann, regular committee as far back as 1948; printing expert.

I also initiated a limited practice of inviting experienced race committeemen who were not NYYC members to serve with us during the Trials. I had come to know **Gaither Scott** and **Ron Ward** during my Annapolis years. Both later joined the club and Gaither became NYYC Race chairman, 1978-1981.

The America's Cup

In the nearly 120 years that the America's Cup had been raced, it had grown into a significant event on a global scale. It held a special place in the U.S. among fans who otherwise cared little about sailing, because it was considered to be the longest winning streak in sports. Since the Schooner *America* won the Cup in 1851, the trophy had lived at the NYYC's clubhouse on West 44th street in Manhattan. It had a hole in its base and was held by a long bolt that went right through the floor. It didn't even leave for Newport when there was competition. It only left the clubhouse to go uptown to Tiffany to be engraved after a Match or for storage, when the clubhouse was closed for the summer, in a bank vault less than a block away. Many challengers had tried to wrest the Cup; all failed. World War II interrupted the triennial sequence of challenge and competition. From 1937 to 1958, while war inflamed the world, and then as humanity healed and recovered, the "gentlemanly sport" of America's Cup racing awaited revision and resurgence.

In 1958, in the first Cup match after the War, *Columbia* successfully defended against *Sceptre*, of Britain's Royal Yacht Squadron, four races-to-none. In 1962, the year I sailed in *Easterner,* the American yacht *Weatherly* defeated the first Australian entry, *Gretel,* 4-1. In those two cycles, in its new, 12-Meter configuration, the America's Cup had firmly re-established itself.

Australia's Royal Sydney Yacht Squadron, with the backing of newspaper potentate Sir Frank Packer, had taken a keen interest in the America's Cup. The first challenge from Down Under by *Gretel* in 1962 awakened the America's Cup community to a new force. Australia returned in 1967 with *Dame Pattie*, and not discouraged, challenged again in 1970 with *Gretel II.* For the first time, in 1970, multiple challenges were accepted and challenger trials were held in Newport. This was expected to make the Cup match more competitive and it eventually did just that.

Chapter 2

Preparations for the 1970 America's Cup began a few short weeks after *Intrepid's* successful defense in 1967. The NYYC received challenges from Australia, England, France, and Greece. Since Australia was the first to challenge and became the "challenger of record" they agreed to stage a series of trial races to be held in Newport. Greece and England eventually withdrew their challenges. *Gretel II*, from Australia, defeated *France* in the first-ever Challenger Trials for the right to challenge for the America's Cup.

In the defense, three American Twelves, *Intrepid, Valiant, and Heritage* raced on Western Long Island Sound in the Preliminary Trials, from June 8 to 12. *Intrepid* had been significantly altered after the 1967 campaign. *Heritage*, her arrival from Florida having been delayed, joined just two races. All of the races were sailed over America's Cup type courses using the new, movable NYYC turning marks later dubbed Barker's Markers. Winds were light, and a large, unpatrolled spectator fleet was a constant source of worry and annoyance. Coast Guard patrol support was not available on Long Island Sound.

The Observation Trials, held off Newport, July 7-18, *Heritage, Intrepid,* and *Valiant* were joined by *Weatherly*, the 1962 Cup defender. Each of the defense candidates was thus able to compete on every race day. It was great for us to be in Newport where we could start gearing up for the main event. *Incredible*, the new

Hatteras-70 chartered as our committee boat, was finally delivered from North Carolina in early July and picked up a lively group of younger race committee members and their children, including mine ages four and seven, for the last leg from New York to Newport.

NEW YORK YACHT CLUB
RACE COMMITTEE

INCREDIBLE

L.O.A. — 70'   DISPL. — 70,000 lb.
BEAM — 18' 7"   DESIGN — J. B. Hargrave
DRAFT — 5'   HULL — Fiberglass
POWER — Twin GM 12V diesels

Built by HATTERAS YACHT
for the NYYC Race Committee
Launched May, 1970 at New Bern, N.C.

Charter arrangements through Bartram & Brackenhoff.

The name INCREDIBLE was given to this yacht by her builders out of affectionate tribute to the memory of the late Willis Slane, a founder of Hatteras and pioneer in the fiberglass boatbuilding industry. Slane, a colorful and sometimes controversial character, used profanity as the situation demanded, like all good sailors. In polite company he learned to substitute "*incredible!*" for just about any four-letter word with the explanation, a favorite story of his, that just such reforms were the reasons fathers sent their sons to Ivy League colleges.

INCREDIBLE is the first Hatteras-70, a stock fiberglass boat that is believed to be the largest of her type and which will be in regular production starting this fall . . . facts which in themselves are rather incredible.

The Final Trial Races to select the America's Cup defender began August 18. After three races *Weatherly* was excused from further participation. After two more races, *Heritage* was eliminated. *Intrepid and Valiant* raced five more times, with the former winning all. On August 30, *Intrepid* became a two-time defender.

For the first time in either a Trial or a Cup contest since the Cup had been revived in 1958, there were protests between the boats for perceived violations of the racing rules. The protests were decided by the NYYC Race Committee, namely myself and my associates, with no appeal to other authorities. The rules used by the NYYC were identical in all important aspects to those in use in sailboat racing throughout the world. As it turned out, the four protests in the Trial races were precursors of things to come and worthwhile training for the Race Committee which, I thought, demonstrated again and again that it was a truly capable group.

The America's Cup races began Tuesday, September 15. The wind was brisk at the start, around 20 knots, and the American defender, *Intrepid*, led from start to finish to win by a 5:52 margin. *Gretel II* lost a man overboard, who had to be recovered, which exaggerated the margin, but the difference in speed between the boats in a good breeze was apparent.

Both *Intrepid* and *Gretel II* filed protests against the other after a rather awkward pre-start confrontation in which *Gretel II* seemed to be trying to prevent *Intrepid* from keeping clear by altering course to prevent the defender from doing so, a tactic called hunting. The Race Committee disallowed both protests since it did not feel either yacht had broken any rules.

At the protest hearing which was quite cordial, both skippers, *Intrepid*'s Bill Ficker and *Gretel II's* Jim Hardy, suggested that a meeting be held with the Race Committee to discuss interpretation of the Racing Rules. We wrote them a note later in the day saying that while we felt "such a discussion might be of benefit to both skippers, it would be inappropriate for the Race Committee to participate." We simply could not put ourselves in a position where a hypothetical situation could be construed to be identical to an actual situation. We needed to be left free to make decisions solely on the basis of the facts found in each particular situation. The request did give some of us pause to wonder what might be ahead. Were both skippers intending to aggressively push the rules to the limits and wanted the race committee to indicate what those limits might be?

In America's Cup racing, in 1970, each vessel was allowed unlimited "lay days" following a completed race or a race being called off for the day. With no reason given, the skipper could signal his unwillingness to start the next day. *Gretel II* did so after the first race. While a lay day request was not out of the ordinary, particularly for the challenger, it was a contributing factor in the mounting pressure we on the Race Committee felt on Sunday.

So there was no race on Wednesday.

There was not enough wind to race on Thursday.

Our usual rule of thumb for starting races on foggy days: We needed to be able to clearly see the buoy end of the starting line, set to be 400 yards in length from the committee boat, during the entire 20-minute starting sequence.

A second race got underway in perhaps a half-mile of visibility at 12:30 on Friday. In a nine knot breeze, *Gretel II* led at the start and by almost two minutes at the first mark. But *Intrepid* sailed lower and faster with a more effective spinnaker on the reaches and had gained a 46 second lead at the third mark. She was still in the lead on the fourth leg when thicker fog descended.

In match racing there is not much point to the race if you are unable to see your opponent. Also, it is dangerous with a large, disorganized spectator fleet crowding the course from all sides. With visibility down to 200 yards or less, the Coast Guard patrol commander, calling from the 380' Coast Guard Cutter *Chase*, implored us to stop the race. After as much delay as we could possibly engineer, we reluctantly did so in the interests of safety.

While there had been any number of races that didn't finish because the time limit expired, this was the very first time in America's Cup history that a race in progress had been *abandoned* which by definition in the racing rules is "one which the race committee declares void at any time after the starting signal and which can be resailed at its discretion."

Over the years, books and magazine articles have quoted the Australians as being critical of our decision, because, first, they thought they were neck and neck or even ahead at the time; and, secondly, the fog wasn't all that thick. Our action has been cited as an example of the NYYC race committee making a decision to benefit its own boat. I provide the detail that follows in order to balance the record.

DIAGRAM OF COURSE

Keep in mind that the America's Cup course had six legs—a triangle followed by windward and leeward legs and then a final beat to the finish for a total distance of 24.3 nautical miles. So the committee boat had to relocate after the start in order to finish the race at the weather mark. Here is the procedure we had followed all summer: By the time the boats were approaching the end of the triangle, we had our anchor up and had positioned ourselves to be able to record the margin at the third mark. We then followed the race up the fourth leg, staying closely astern and roughly halfway between the two boats.

As the visibility deteriorated, we were able to follow the boats on *Incredible*'s radar. We were keeping track and we knew that it was close but that *Intrepid* was indeed ahead. We had one of our most experienced committee members, Charlie Morgan, aboard the *Chase* and we knew the ship had slowed down and essentially stopped trying to keep the race course clear. We were in touch with the defender and challenger tenders (which had radar) and asked the tenders to report if and when they lost visual contact with each one's sailing vessel. A few minutes later, the tenders did so, almost simultaneously.

The previous winter I had given some thought to the possibility of having to abandon a race, even though it had never happened before. We discussed it at meetings, but when the Sailing Instructions were printed they were silent on the subject. After an incident in the Challenger Trials in August when *France* became lost in fog and retired from the race, we prepared the following Notice which was issued the day before the Match began at the Captain's Meeting:

"The Sailing Instructions in no way inhibit the power of the Race Committee to *abandon* a race under Rule 5.1(b), but in accordance with the Conditions, a course will not be shortened. Notice of *abandonment* will be given to your tenders over VHF channel 6...."

At that moment, we felt blessed to have the procedure spelled out and available.

Finally, an incredibly detailed recollection 42 years after the fact from *Intrepid* tactician Steve Van Dyck: "*Gretel II* was abeam to leeward 5.5 boat lengths (stadimeter reading) on the fourth leg when the race was abandoned. We had really started to move on them as we had a little more pressure filling in with the fog. She was right on the edge of being totally beyond our visibility. Upon abandonment I promptly said to Bill Ficker 'it is a damn good thing we are ahead.' To which he said 'boy are you right!' We were employing a tight cover at the time and would not have let her go off in the fog to 'strike gold.' I was very alarmed at racing in the fog with the extreme danger of the spectator fleet milling around out of control and not being able to avoid a damaging collision."

Following the abandoned-because-of-fog Race 2, *Gretel II* called for another lay day.

After nearly a week of racing, only one race had been completed. There had been two lay days, one windless day, and fog. Even though circumstances were completely beyond our control, the Committee and I were frustrated and starting to feel somewhat pressured. If all of the fits and failed/postponed/canceled starts were not enough, the expectations of the media horde and the general public was becoming greater and greater. The next race day, Sunday, we knew we had to push really hard to complete Race 2.

A crew of eleven men sailed the 12-Meter boats. All were amateurs who were college students or had day jobs in their regular lives. Three on the foredeck handled headsails and halyards; four amidships worked headsail sheets and winches; a man aft for the main sheet, a navigator, tactician and skipper. The skipper was the master of his yacht and crew, directing everything that happens in his charge. The tactician's jobs were many: watch the other boat, watch for wind shifts, and analyze the boat's performance. In *Intrepid,* the 27-year-old tactician Steve Van Dyck had an additional job when sailing close hauled. The skipper, because of her very low, bendy boom could not see to leeward. He steered on the windward side. If the competitor was to leeward, Ficker relied entirely on what Van Dyck told him. During the long summer's campaign a totally trusting relationship had developed between the two and they thought alike. Some of the time they used non-verbal ways to communicate. Gestures and body English were common.

Twelve-meter yachts did not actually sail from their berths in Newport. They were towed out 12 miles by their tenders to an area near the special America's Cup Buoy, which formed one end of the starting line. During the tow, the crew typically relaxed below deck, and ate lunch.

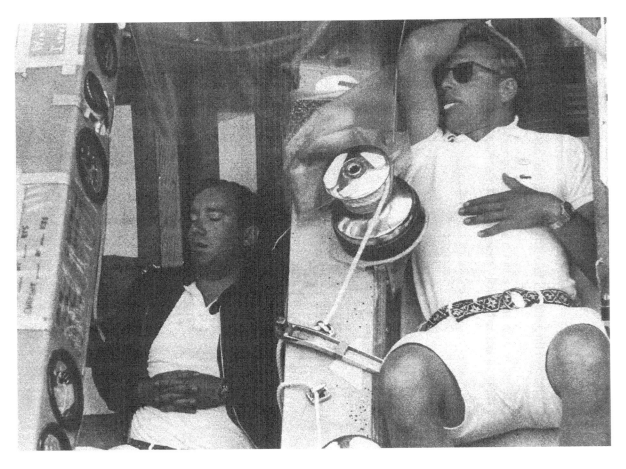

Taking a nap during the tow out, *Intrepid*'s Peter Wilson (left) and Stephen Van Dyck

In September, in New England, yellow jackets, the common name for a genus of predatory wasp, reach maturity, and become particularly aggressive. They also seek sweet, sugary food sources. Below deck, during lunch on the tow out for the Sunday start, an opportunistic yellow jacket (following open cans of Coca-Cola) applied its love to Steve Van Dyck's right cheek. To people who are not allergic to bee stings, a yellow jacket's bite is a painful, usually rude, experience. If the victim is allergic, the pain is just the same, but medical attention is immediately necessary.

Van Dyck was not allergic. Or so he thought. Within a few minutes, however, his face began to swell. His breathing became shallow. He began to sweat. The crew aboard *Intrepid* quickly recognized a medical emergency and called the Coast Guard on VHF. Within minutes, a helicopter hoisted the stricken tactician from *Intrepid* and delivered him to the hospital in Newport. (Van Dyck was treated and released after about an hour and a half.)

An improbable bee sting and Van Dyck was suddenly gone. But the Intrepid Syndicate, which did things thoroughly, had thought about emergency replacement personnel. Toby Tobin, who had navigated *Intrepid* in 1967 and held a similar position on rival *Valiant* in 1970 was in the spectator fleet and immediately transferred to *Intrepid*. He took the place of Peter Wilson, the navigator, who was moved into the tactician's spot. The impact on *Intrepid*'s decision making appears to have been minimal. Steve Van Dyck has always maintained that he would have made exactly the same call as Peter Wilson did.

The wind that Sunday, September 20, was light and very variable. The conditions were really not suitable for an America's Cup race, but as mentioned earlier we were under great pressure to sail the race. It was Sunday afternoon of the first weekend of the America's Cup match; there were at least 1,000 boats in the spectator fleet; Coast Guard and Navy ships were busy in the area; the sky was full of helicopters carrying news crews; and only one race thus far had been finished. If it had been a "normal" day, I feel quite certain we would not have raced.

Ideally, the starting line should be perpendicular or square to the direction of the wind so that one end is not favored over the other. The line is created by the America's Cup Buoy and the committee boat, *Incredible*, anchored approximately 400 yards apart. We did have the ability to reposition the committee boat and often did so; on this day, however, the wind continually shifted around. Just as it seemed to settle, it would shift again. So we repeatedly postponed the start and hoped for better, but alas, there was little improvement. Regardless, we decided to race. Starting at 2:10 was as late in the day as the Conditions allowed. Even with as few as two minutes remaining in the starting sequence,

Bill Fanning and I were considering postponing and calling it a day. It was that bad.

At the start the wind was 6 knots from 238 degrees. Both yachts wanted to start at the heavily- favored committee boat end of the line and gain the right-hand side of the course where more wind could be expected to fill in. This circumstance gave us a perfect view, at very close range, of the events that transpired at the start of Race 2.

The Committee and the skippers later agreed that: "Prior to the starting signal (a pair of 12-gauge signaling cannons fired simultaneously) both yachts were approaching the starting line on the starboard tack. *Intrepid* was to windward and rapidly overtaking *Gretel II* from astern. *Intrepid* was on a close hauled course to pass astern of the Committee Boat. *Gretel II* was slowly luffing.

"After the starting signal and before the yachts had cleared the starting line, *Gretel II* continued her slow luff until she was above a close hauled course. During this maneuver the yachts became overlapped and converged. *Gretel II*'s bow struck *Intrepid* just abaft the chainplates on the port side."

Gretel II lost her false bow in the collision, but no other damage was done to either vessel. One piece of the bow landed on *Intrepid*'s deck. The piece was saved by the crew; later to be made into a plaque for Bill Ficker with an inscription indicating that it had been "deposited aboard" *Intrepid.*

(The Australians have complained for years that while they might agree the Rules were applied correctly, we got the facts wrong because *Intrepid* was not close hauled. I agree that it might have been more correct to say "*Intrepid* was close hauled with her sheets eased," but as has been pointed out many times, this is irrelevant to the application of the rules that govern the situation.)

One of my thoughts as the events unfolded in front of us was: when is *Gretel II* going to come off? She must have lost her steering. It was a chaotic scene out there. Helicopters clattered overhead. *Incredible* had a definite roll, and lurched about in the leftover slop created by the spectator boats.

In addition to the NYYC Race Committee, also onboard the committee boat were my father, who was there as my guest, and Richard A. "Dicko" Dickson, the heavy-set, jolly commodore of the Royal Sydney Yacht Squadron as official observer for RSYS, whose yacht had just collided with *Intrepid*.

Almost immediately, I understood the reality of the situation. Rules had been violated. Protests would be filed because there was contact. The Race Committee would have to make a decision. We were witnesses. Less than a minute after the start I asked my Dad to accompany Dicko below. Once the Committee had some privacy, I asked, "What did you see?"

Starting signal has been made, gun smoke is visible. *Intrepid*, at right, going twice as fast.

Gretel II continues to come up, her jib luffing

Just after contact, 15 seconds after starting signal. This photo and one on cover taken approx. same time

Chapter 3

I n a quick conference, we agreed that:

- We saw *Gretel II* impact *Intrepid*.

- We saw *Gretel II* on an above-close-hauled course at the time of impact.

- We saw both boats immediately display protest flags.

Intrepid pulled ahead at the start, but *Gretel II* turned out to be faster in light air and did overtake *Intrepid* on the fifth leg to win Race 2 by a margin of 1:07, guaranteeing for me a situation I had been worrying about for months but which I could do nothing to change. The following is quoted from the Conditions, immediately above the signatures of Commodores Dickson of the RSYS and Ewing of the NYYC:

22. Decisions of the Race Committee: The decisions of the Race Committee of the New York Yacht Club in all matters pertaining to the Racing Rules shall be final and there shall be no appeal therefrom.

After the race, both *Gretel II* and *Intrepid* called for a lay day the next day, Monday, Sept. 21.

Both *Intrepid* and *Gretel II* filed protests that evening.

Even though there had not been a protest in an America's Cup race since 1934 and the last protest before that was in 1895, as early as mid-Winter 1969-1970, I began to worry that a protest situation could bring into question the NYYC Race Committee's neutrality and appearance of fairness should we have to rule against the challenging (non-American) yacht. After discussing the idea with Harry Anderson, I decided to consult with F. Gregg Bemis, who was a greatly respected elder statesman and perhaps the world's foremost expert on racing rules. A Harvard man who had homes in Concord and Cohasset, Massachusetts, Bemis was not a member of the NYYC. After some gentle arm twisting, he agreed that he would be available to us should we need him.

Early Monday morning, I called Bemis at home and asked him if he would like to come to Newport to sit in on the hearing. He told me was glad to do so, but he had studied the photos in the newspaper, seen the smoke of the starting cannon to confirm the start, and believed it was not very complicated. Certainly, we agreed, *Intrepid* was in the vulnerable "barging" position. But if the gap is big enough, there is nothing illegal about barging. If the room was there, she was entitled to take it and *Gretel II* was forbidden from sailing above close hauled, once the starting gun had fired, to deny *Intrepid* passage.

At the hearing Monday morning aboard *Incredible* docked at King's Park near the Ida Lewis YC, Bill Ficker, *Intrepid's* skipper, and Martin Visser from *Gretel II* presented their versions of the incident and their interpretation of the applicable rules. There were aerial photographs from multiple angles to choose from, they had made diagrams and used miniature model boats. Visser called his skipper Jim Hardy as a witnesses and Ficker called two *Intrepid* crewmen. Such Witnesses from the same boat have little impact since the jury knows full well that they have been coached on what to say. We made a procedural error by allowing Jim Hardy to stay at the hearing. After he gave his testimony, he should have departed as the *Intrepid* witnesses did. Our committee always took great pride in thoroughness, doing things correctly, and professionalism. We wanted as much information as either side was willing to give us even though we had seen it. The hearing was civil; all of the Committee members wore jacket and tie on the claustrophobic after deck. No one raised his voice. After 45 minutes, the hearing adjourned.

After we had discussed and then drafted the decision to disqualify *Gretel II*, I appointed Race Committee members Bill Fanning and Jim Carroll, two of our most knowledgeable on the Rules, to be "Devil's Advocates." Their job was to try and find holes in our decision. They removed themselves to another area of the boat and deliberated for at least another half hour or so. They confirmed the decision to disqualify *Gretel II*.

The NYYC flag officers were nearby at the same dock, but they never talked to us or tried to influence us in any way. They learned of our actions after we had implemented them.

We found that *Gretel II* had violated Rule 42.1(e), which states that after the starting signal she could not deprive *Intrepid* of room to pass the required side of the committee boat by sailing above close hauled. She was not only above close hauled, but a case could have been made that at the point of contact she was on port tack. See the photos. (Young *Gretel II* port tailer John Bertrand, who in 1983 lifted the Cup as skipper of *Australia II*, had released the jib sheet.) Rule 42.1(e) overrides any of the rules under which *Gretel II* protested and thus *Gretel II*'s protest was disallowed.`

We delivered the decision in writing to each of the Syndicates by early afternoon. *Intrepid*'s crew, who Peter Wilson recalls had no doubt about the outcome, wanted to know what took so long. Sir Frank Packer received his messages by sending his aid Mike Ramsden, who became a top TV newsman in Australia, to our dock. We saw a lot of Ramsden in coming days.

Shortly thereafter, at the Newport Armory on Thames Street, we announced the decision, which was still not public, to the press. I was really not prepared for what followed. Naively, as it turned out, I trusted that with the clarity of the situation and the obvious rules violation we would have no problems. Somehow I thought our personal integrity would be unquestioned. Three hundred press credentials had been issued; the crush of reporters and onlookers exceeded anything I anticipated. No police were evident. The tension in the room was palpable.

Bob Bavier, a colleague at *Yachting*, who had successfully defended the Cup as skipper of *Constellation* in 1964, a former president of North American Yacht Racing Union and a recognized expert on the Racing Rules, was the moderator at the press conference. I read the decision, which was actually fairly dense legalese, and as soon as I finished with the word "disallowed," from the back of the room, Martin Visser, age 45, *Gretel II's* aggressive helmsman, cried out, "NO, NO, NO!"

The Chairman announcing the protest decision

The packed press conference at the Newport Armory

Visser was not your typical yachtsman, and I thought he might attack me. As I left the podium, when I still could not sense any police presence, I was glad to see nearby my friend Westy Saltonstall, a former college linebacker and rugby player who was 6'2", 225 lb., and had been a grinder on *Valiant* that summer. I headed toward Westy and trusted that Visser would not try anything with him around.

The press corps erupted with questions. Most of the reporters did not know anything about sailing or the Racing Rules. Baseball writers, they knew baselines, but not the layline, and their questions revealed their ignorance. Bavier tried to consolidate the questions. Soon enough the questions became repetitive, and we realized that explaining the technicalities of match racing to people who didn't know the difference between port and starboard was impossible.

We concluded the press conference in less than an hour, without incident, and planned for Race 3, to be held Tuesday. Our decision had set in motion an international tsunami of telegrams, mail and criticism headed directly for the Race Committee and the New York Yacht Club. It was fueled by Sir Frank who knew full well how to manipulate the press. Every reporter on earth thrives on controversy. It looked like a "hometown" decision. The hungry reporters had just what they needed.

Sir Frank also kept up the pressure on us with a series of letters, delivered by Mike Ramsden, attempting to re-open the Race 2 hearing. The first was delivered on September 25 after two more races had been completed and the series stood at 3-1 *Intrepid*. In recent years I have come to understand that although Sir Frank signed the letters, Jim Hardy was the force behind them.

The late Robert C. MacArthur wrote a wonderful book, *Room at the Mark*, that includes a history of the racing rules. Rob and I had become acquainted after I moved back to the Boston area in 1972. I introduced him to Gregg Bemis and they soon became fast friends. Gregg wrote the Foreword to Rob's book and introduced him to G. Sambrooke Sturgess, the leading British rules authority who, with Gregg, had been the driving force behind racing rules development since the 1960's. Jim Hardy had contacted Sturgess as you will learn below.

According to Rob: "Packer wrote asking that the hearing be reopened, citing a portion of rule 68 that states: 'The race committee shall allow any omission in the details...to be remedied at a later time.' The letter went on to say that the omission they wanted to put before the Committee was the 'alleged violation' by *Intrepid* of rule 42.3(a)(ii), the two-boat-length determinative."

Rob MacArthur, exaggerating somewhat, continues: "The entire yachting world, let alone the race committee, was astonished! What in heaven's name was Packer talking about? The anti-barging rule had been used in the United States and Canada for 22 years and in the rest of the world for 11 years. There had never been any restriction on a windward yacht establishing an overlap....Any intention by the rules makers to link the new determinative to the anti-barging rule would have been utterly senseless. The one was addressed to the inside yacht, establishing the conditions under which she would be entitled to room at a mark. The other was addressed to the outside (leeward) yacht, telling her that she need give no room at a starting mark."

(I was age 10 when the anti-barging rule arrived and I distinctly recall its provisions being drummed into me by a Pleon YC sailing instructor, over and over: "Once the gun goes, you must head off. You can't squeeze out the windward boat by sailing above close hauled.")

Gretel II's afterguard claimed that *Intrepid* had established an overlap illegally. Back to Rob: "It was a novel argument. Harold Vanderbilt had been correct in saying that his anti-barging rule would not cause any confusion or misunderstanding, because the situations while starting and at mark roundings were so different. Indeed, it quickly became one of the best understood rules in the entire code. Many people had been disqualified under the rule, of course....because they took the risk that sufficient room would be there and were wrong...."

After confirming our opinion with Gregg Bemis, we replied to Sir Frank's letter the same day, which was a layday taken by *Intrepid,* anticipating light air: "The request introduces neither new evidence nor arguments on the rules not previously considered..." Perhaps to be polite and because we thought this would be the end of it, we decided not to address the question of whether the hearing could be reopened at all.

Hardy did not give up. He reached Sambrooke Sturgess in England who had just spent a full day racing on the Norfolk Broads and had not been closely following what was taking place in Newport. Sturgess declined an invitation to come to Newport but undoubtedly felt some pressure to aid a British Commonwealth cause. After what Bemis says were three or four hours of drafting, he dispatched a non-committal cable [to Hardy], implying support, that concluded, "there is no case law on this question but it deserves consideration."

On September 26 the fog came in thick and we postponed without ever leaving the harbor. *Intrepid* again asked for a layday because of the light air forecast.

Mike Ramsden appeared at our gangway on September 27 with a letter quoting the Sturgess cable and again asking for a reopening of the Race 2 hearing. Since it was a layday, we were not pressed for time to issue another response. And the press was not involved, thank goodness. The letter exchanges between Sir Frank and me were not made public until release of the 1970 NYYC Race Committee Report in mid November.

Rob MacArthur on 'deserves consideration:' "The question raised in this instance was legitimate and it deserved an answer. That means interpretation by some authority. The NYYC Race Committee was in a bind there, for it could not approach a higher authority [under the Conditions]. It did the only thing it could do, which was to consult a member of the International Yacht Racing Union Racing Rules Committee, Gregg Bemis, who could be counted on to know what that body's intention was....

"The Committee was in the awkward position of having to say, in one breath, that it could not entertain an appeal, and then, in the next, rendering what amounted to an appeals decision by standing on its earlier interpretation..."

But we are getting ahead of ourselves. People with opinions everywhere were jumping to passionate conclusions.

Five visible crewmembers work on *Intrepid* during a fog delay at the dock

Chapter 4

Public opinion was against us in many places. Even before the races had begun, the *(Sydney) Sunday Times,* accused the "gentlemen of the New York Yacht Club of juggling the rules to make things tougher for the challenger." *The New York Times'* columnist Robert Lipsyte was sent to Newport and penned a decidedly anti-establishment "Sports of the Times" column about the America's Cup, and by extension, the New York YC, on September 18, in which he called me the "standard bearer of a dying, repressive order."

I did not know Lipsyte. He pounced on the America's Cup as "controversial" fodder for something to write about, and he did a good job of getting under my skin. The column and its provocative language was a further indication of how "big" the Cup had become. I never should have talked to Lipsyte and thereafter did my best to stay away from the non-yachting press. Bob Bavier and I continued to be available to those we knew, particularly those writers who understood the rules.

The day after Race 2, the telegrams began to pour in; those critical of the ruling greatly outnumbered those in support. Once the Western Union men found *Incredible,* it seemed like they were there every hour on the half hour.

More than a few came from Australians.

From Barrie Gainford, a self-described ordinary Australian: "Decision to disqualify our yacht dismays and frightens all decent American loving Australians. God help America if your bad sportsmanship is national."

G. Thomas and C.A. Potham, of Adelaide, Australia, proclaimed that the decision would "go down in international yachting history as the most blatant demonstration of outright bias and favoritism expressed by any sporting body."

R.L. Falkner, a member of the Royal Brighton Yacht Squadron, in Victoria, Australia registered his great disappointment and surprise the [the Committee's] bad sportsmanship.

Petitions arrived: Susan Saunders, age 14, of Sydney, Australia gathered signatures from fifty-seven schoolmates in a "Petition against Injustice."

The twenty-seven 9th grade boys of the Marist Brothers Innisfail School, Queensland, Australia signed a letter "protesting strongly against the rules governing the running of the America's Cup."

The Fourth grade class at the Templestone Primary School, in Victoria, Australia, sent 22 individually written and signed letters questioning why *Gretel II* was disqualified.

"Relax fellas — I'm recalling the Sixth Fleet from the Middle East."

While the Australian comments were understandable, the opinions that came from all across America were stunning.

One Joann O'Neill, of the International Lightning Fleet in Wisconsin, sneered, "Congratulations to the New York Yacht Club Race Committee for managing to give American Yachting the blackest name in its history."

Francis McGuire, of New London, CT commanded us to rerun the second race to preserve the luster of the Cup and avoid ridicule of the world.

A spectator captain from Waltham, MA opined, "Awarding unearned victory destroys all respect for your organization."

H. A. Baud, "congratulated" us, from Mill Valley, CA, on making a great many yachtsmen ashamed of being American.

G. Stewart of Toronto, sarcastically cried, "Oh you poor prince."

A few letters acknowledged the correctness of our decision. Most came from people who knew the rules:

The Newport (RI) YC "commended" me and the Committee for the outstanding performance displayed throughout the entire 1970 America's Cup series." And the Lightning Fleet in Northport, NY, expressed its opinion that the "Committee was entirely correct in the interpretation and administration of the rule."

NYYC member, E.G. Moran, of Darien, CT wrote: "Congratulations to you and your committee on a difficult job well done." Among the many other members who took the time to write were: Townie Horner, Fenny Johnson, Vic Romagna, Tom Hume, Bill Luders, Bob Blumenstock, Dick Nye, and Percy Chubb. The membership in general seemed to understand we were "taking one" for the club and were appreciative. The Conditions made us the Jury and there was no other way about it.

The written letters tended to be more deliberate and thoughtful than the telegrams (which should be thought of as 20th century forebears of email.) Patrick Cowan, of Waterloo, Ontario, recommended an international judicial body for America's Cup protests. He went on to suggest that if the Cup is not defended with sportsmanship, it is not worth the challenge." Alan Mather, of Wilton CT, was angry because the "real loser was not *Gretel II* but fair play and sportsmanship."

We sent hundreds of replies, but could not respond to each and every letter and telegram individually, as many did not have return addresses. We often enclosed a reprint copy of Bob Bavier's article, "The Protest," which appeared in the November, 1970 issue of *Yachting.* An enclosed preprinted card read:

"With regard to your communication pertaining to the protest at the start of the second America's Cup race: We are enclosing material reprinted from the Nov.'70 issue of *Yachting* Magazine. We hope that you will be able to find the answers to your questions therein.

Race Committee,
New York Yacht Club"

One of the most intriguing telegrams, dated September 23 (Tuesday), was signed by forty-one directors of athletics at colleges in the Eastern Collegiate Athletic Conference (which includes the Ivy League). They "urged in interest highest American sportsmanship second race be called quote no race unquote and be rerun." The telegram received considerable publicity and seemed to have definite influence on non-sailing readers of the sports pages.

In December, I finally replied: "During the football season recently concluded I have been keeping track of the games in which fourth-period touchdowns nullified by penalties changed the outcome. I would like to ask the ECAC Athletic Directors who signed "The" telegram if they would be willing to void these games and replay them at some early opportunity." I asked the ECAC to retract the statement made in the telegram, and suggested that many of the individuals who signed the telegram would now welcome the opportunity to disassociate themselves from what was certainly an emotional, rather than logical reaction to the outcome of Race 2.

In January I received a sincere, personal apology from Robert "Scotty" Whitelaw, associate commissioner of the ECAC "for embarrassment caused through the telegram sent to Newport..." The letter recognized that it would be impossible to rerun the race under the rules of yacht racing, and he also acknowledged his group's rather questionable judgment in signing the telegram. Whitelaw was also writing on behalf of Assistant Commissioner Andy Geiger who later became athletic director at Ohio State.

By December, some people had begun to acknowledge that the Committee's decision was correct. Commodore B.H. Loxton, the Naval Attaché at the Australian Embassy in Washington, DC, sent me a 14-page, closely spaced typewritten letter that contained the observations of Rowley Morgan, a member of the Royal Sydney YS who was regarded as the top rules authority in Australia. Morgan said that he remains convinced that the NYYC's Race Committee acted honestly and without prejudice. Later in the missive, Loxton related that Morgan believed helmsman Visser's tactics on the starting line to be questionable at best.

Morgan stated that there can be no doubt that the disqualification of *Gretel II* was a severe shock not only to the Australians, but to the majority of townspeople in Newport. At the end of the letter, Loxton himself admits to his change of opinion in favor of the ruling.

Loxton included a copy of a memorandum to the Australian Ambassador to the United States stating that, after much review, there was "no longer any doubt whatsoever concerning the rightness of the Committee's decision." It was gratifying to hear, finally, of rational thoughts, overcoming the ill-informed.

Oh yes, amid the torrent of press criticism and mail, there were three more Cup races. *Intrepid* won Races 3 and 5 to successfully defend the America's Cup, 4-1.

As I have said many times, it is regrettable that the Race 2 protest clouds, even still to this day, what was a very strong Australian challenge and a series superbly sailed by Bill Ficker and his crew with a boat that was not as fast as *Gretel II* in many of the conditions encountered.

Chapter 5

I spent considerable time during the winter of 1970-1971 defending the NYYC and our ruling. There seemed to be real interest in my account of events, and I lectured at least a dozen times on what I called the "rubber chicken" circuit. ("Rubber chicken" being standard catered fare at most yacht clubs' annual banquets.) I spoke about and explained the decision to disqualify *Gretel II*. The audiences for the most part were knowledgeable sailing people who understood as I explained the technicalities. But this was yet another aspect of the job for which I had no training.

Fortunately for me, Walter Cronkite of CBS News, a NYYC member, came to the rescue. We made an eight-minute film with aerial footage and his familiar voice narrating. It was the opening segment of my program and I didn't have to say anything. The audience just listened to Walter.

Then I stressed my own feelings:

- Protests are a necessary evil.

- The racing rules are designed to prevent collisions and allow yachts to follow recognized traffic patterns so that close competition is possible.

- The rules were never intended to be used as an offensive weapon to "tag out" an opponent.

I confirmed that nobody at the NYYC, including the race committee, wanted to see *Gretel II* disqualified and that it would have been nice if the club or the Intrepid Syndicate could have offered to re-sail the race. "But can you imagine," I said, "the precedent that would have been set in the sailing world. It would make rules enforcement meaningless and create a code that said, in effect, it is permissible to foul just as long as you hurt yourself more while doing so." That seemed to resonate with most audiences.

In arguing for an International Jury in the future, a favorite line was to quote the Supreme Court's Louis Brandeis: "Justice must not only be done, it must <u>appear</u> to be done."

While not being in agreement, it is impossible not to be amused by one of Sir Frank's most memorable comments, "An Australian skipper protesting to the New York YC is like a husband complaining to his mother-in-law about his wife."

The dinner-speeches made at least some difference. In January 1971, Rear Admiral Colin Dunlop, Royal Navy, admitted in a letter that he was "fully convinced of the fairness of the Committee's decision." He had attended a glittering private dinner in Washington, DC hosted by Carter Brown and Juan Cameron at which I made a presentation.

The controversy about perceived home-team bias reached high levels in American-Australian diplomatic relations. James S. Hellen, a citizen in Wayne, NJ wrote the American Ambassador to Australia, Walter L. Rice, expressing displeasure with the process and the outcome of the Race 2 protest. Mr. Hellen sent a copy of the letter to Vice-president Spiro Agnew. The Ambassador copied both Agnew and me in his reply to Mr. Hellen, in which he acknowledged how it was "regrettable that the contest for the America's Cup generated so much controversy." But after seeing and understanding the photographs, most Australians "appeared to acknowledge that the Committee's decision was correct."

Amazingly, active conversation about the Race 2 protest has never stopped among yacht-racing rules specialists and yacht-racing historians. To a large extent this is fueled by the Australians, particularly Jim Hardy, who continues to complain that we had the facts wrong despite what we saw with our own eyes and more photographic evidence than just about any other protest incident in yacht racing history. I have said this before and I will say it again, those in the cockpit of *Gretel II* had a very poor working knowledge of the Racing Rules. In recent years, I have learned from other Cup historians that some of the younger *Gretel II* crew members felt the same way and were embarrassed about it.

Two significant legacies of the Race 2 controversies survived:

First, that a race could be abandoned at the discretion of the Race Committee was codified. Recall, no race in the 120-year history of America's Cup had ever been abandoned. In what was the first Race 2, the "fog race" on Friday, September 18, we were forced to stop the race. Nearly the exact same language that was so useful that day entered the America's Cup Conditions of 1974.

Most important to me was creation of an international jury. At America's Cup Committee meetings to which I was invited, I advocated strongly for an international jury in future Cup matches. True, there had been no need for an international jury, or a jury of any kind, because protests had not been thought to be part America's Cup racing.

This thinking had even been articulated in the 1934 NYYC Race Committee report:

"We are reliably informed that the International character of the race alone prevented *Rainbow* from protesting at the start, it having been agreed between Commodore Harold S. Vanderbilt and the America's Cup Committee, prior to the commencement of the races, that as a matter of policy, protests should be avoided." The committee was referring to a pre-start situation in which the challenger, *Endeavour*, clearly fouled *Rainbow*.

Oh, how events forced us to consider new mechanisms.

In an October, 1970 memorandum, I wrote: "The Race Committee feels quite strongly that future Cup protests should be decided by some sort of neutral jury. There appears to be no other way to protect the Club from the slurs of the uninitiated and unfair charges of partiality. It would be nice to say that we don't care what the outside world thinks, but the America's Cup has become a symbol of national pride far beyond sailing circles. We must take this into consideration."

Evidence of internal reluctance to cede the power to adjudicate protests is found in a letter from Clayton Ewing, Commodore of the NYYC, to Gregg Bemis, the rules expert. Ewing confided that he was struggling with the problem of how to avoid the "unfortunate impression" that the NYYC makes the rules and arbitrarily interprets them. He continued, almost transparently revealing his pride in the NYYC's people and capabilities, "Obviously, one easy out would be to have an independent committee to decide protests, but as one thinks that possibility through, you begin to run into negative aspects that may be just as important as the positive."

Eventually, following extensive internal debate, reality defeated pride, and for the 1974 Match, the following language appeared for the first time in the Conditions:

22. **In addition there shall be an International Jury composed of not less than three individuals who are not nationals of the countries of either contesting Club, which shall act on protests and interpretations of the racing rules deriving therefrom. The decisions of the International Jury shall be final and there shall be no appeal therefrom.**

With the end of my term as Race Committee Chairman in 1971, I joined the Auxiliary Committee, as past Race Committee chairmen often do, and served in various roles in the 1974, 1977, 1980, and 1983 America's Cup matches. It was great fun to participate in the running of the races without the burden of the Chairman's responsibilities.

I did limited judging at major international events in the years that followed 1970 and chaired the 1990 and 1992 Newport to Bermuda ocean races, but my real pleasure had been a return to racing and cruising my own sailboats.

The memories of September 20, 1970 and the great committee members with whom I served will never be far from the surface. Together we made a decision that needed to be made and stuck with it.

Moment of impact: from a rarely seen angle to leeward.

OFFICIAL COMMITTEE DECISION: 2ND RACE PROTEST

PROTESTS OF "GRETEL II" AND "INTREPID"

Yacht *Gretel II* protested yacht *Intrepid* for violation of Rules 37.1, 37.2, and 40 in the second America's Cup Race on September 20, 1970. Yacht *Intrepid* protested yacht *Gretel II* for violation of Rule 42.1(e).

Facts

Prior to the starting signal, both yachts were approaching the starting line on the starboard tack. *Intrepid* was to windward and rapidly overtaking *Gretel II* from astern. *Intrepid* was on a close-hauled course to pass astern of the committee boat. *Gretel II* was slowly luffing.

After the starting signal and before the yachts had cleared the starting line, *Gretel II* continued her slow luff until she was above a close-hauled course. During this maneuver the yachts became overlapped and converged. *Gretel II*'s bow struck *Intrepid* just abaft of the chainplates on the port side.

Decision

Both yachts were approaching the starting line to start within the intent of Rule 42.1(e). Prior to the starting signal, *Gretel II* was under no obligation to give *Intrepid* room to pass to leeward of the committee boat. After the starting signal, however, *Gretel II* acquired an obligation, as soon as the yachts were overlapped, not to deprive *Intrepid* of room to pass on the required side of the committee boat by sailing above close hauled.

Had *Gretel II* fulfilled her obligation to fall off to a close-hauled course under Rule 42.1(e) *Intrepid* would have had room to pass between *Gretel II* and the committee boat.

Therefore, *Gretel II* is disqualified for infringement of Rule 42.1(e).

Since the above Rule is part of Section E—Rules of Exception and Special Application, it overrides any conflicting rule of Part IV which precedes it, except the rules of Section A—Rules Which Always Apply. Rules 37.1, 37.2, and 40 under which *Gretel II* protested are part of Section C which precedes Section E and are therefore overridden. *Gretel II*'s protest is disallowed.

B. Devereux Barker III
Chairman

Author's Note

Most of what has now been brought together within these pages has been with me for over 40 years. So one might ask, why did it not see the light of day sooner? Primary reason: At the time, 1970, I was on the editorial staff of *Yachting* magazine and it just did not seem appropriate to me or to my employer. Within two years I had left journalism, attended business school and landed a job in the insurance business that lasted 36 years...all with the same firm. Except for business letters and proposals, my writing essentially stopped.

Over the years, I have remained close to the people, history and traditions of the America's Cup as a member of the Selection Committee of the America's Cup Hall of Fame (www.herreshoff.org/achof). I have been a member since it started in 1992 and was pleased to chair the Selection Committee for four years. Its meetings have produced some of the most fascinating sailing conversations I have ever heard. The

Selection Committee is now a truly international body, fully representing the countries that have challenged for the Cup, currently and in the past. I have traveled as far as Auckland, New Zealand and Valencia, Spain for Hall of Fame Induction Ceremonies.

One individual, Gary Jobson who I only knew slightly before he joined the Selection Committee (and then had to depart for two years so he himself could be elected), has said to me a number of times that I should write this book. I doubt there is a single individual who has studied the start of Race 2 more than Gary. He seems to weave the aerial shots of it into all of his films. Another individual who got me going, my nephew John Fiske, knew nothing at all about the incident when he asked me casually one day if I knew of any writing projects. He has been around boats for much of his life but he has never raced sailboats. John, who teaches writing at the college level, has many articles and two books to his credit. His tasks were to sort through my files, make an outline and write the rough initial drafts of most chapters. So Gary and John receive full credit for getting me cranked up after all these years.

Assistance was also received from three other current ACHoF Selection Committee members: England's leading yachting writer Bob Fisher, the renowned author John Rousmaniere and the encyclopedic Steve Tsuchiya, whose fascination with the Cup has led him to travel the world interviewing participants. Bob has ongoing contact with Jim Hardy and was thus able to confirm several long-held Aussie viewpoints as well as, at least to me, introduce a new one. The attempts to re-open the protest hearing ended when Sir Frank said, according to Hardy, "You may not agree, Jim, but you must accept.

John Rousmaniere, who was my predecessor as HoF chairman, was kind enough to read the manuscript and made a number of worthwhile suggestions I was able to incorporate. John was also a *Yachting* staff man early in his career but we just missed overlapping.

Manchester-By-The-Sea, MA
February, 2013

Sources:

Report of the Race Committee, New York Yacht Club, 1934 and 1970.
Yachting magazine, numerous articles and issues, 1963 to 1971.
Room at the Mark, Robert C. MacArthur, The Yacht Owners Register Inc., 1991
An Absorbing Interest, Bob Fisher, John Wiley & Sons Ltd., 2007
The New York Yacht Club, A History 1844-2008, John Rousmaniere, NYYC and Seapoint Books.

Conversations (including email exchanges) with:

Bill Ficker
Stephen Van Dyck
Peter Wilson
Carolyn Wilson
Roger Vaughan
Bill Foulk
Bob Fisher
David Elwell
Jory Hinman
Chris Wick
Westy Saltonstall

Photo credits:

Dan Nerney, front and back covers, page 47
Mystic Seaport, Rosenfeld Collection, pages 4, 6
John Hopf, pages 2, 18, 19, 20, 21
Stephen Lafleur, page 29
T. R. Hearsum, page 33

18832069R00030

Made in the USA
Charleston, SC
23 April 2013